Having the Time of My Life

Bayou Publishing

Having the Time of My Life

by

Helen Smith Owen

Having the Time of My Life
Copyright © 2024—Helen Smith Owen
ALL RIGHTS RESERVED UNDER U.S.,
PAN-AMERICAN, AND INTERNATIONAL
COPYRIGHT CONVENTIONS

All Scripture references are from the *Holy Bible, King James Version,* public domain.

Bayou Publishing, a division of McDougal & Associates, is dedicated to spreading the Gospel of the Lord Jesus Christ to as many people as possible in the shortest time possible.

Published by:

Bayou Publishing
www.ThePublishedWord.com

ISBN: 978-1-950398-83-6

Printed on demand in the U.S., the U.K. and Australia
For Worldwide Distribution

Dedication

This book is dedicated to my family:

My late husband, Craig. My life would have taken a very different turn had I not married him.

My daughter, Kelly Noel Amussen, who has been on this journey with me since the beginning.

My three brothers and two sisters.

My kitty cats, Melissa and Meela, and my dog, Cookie. They kept me sane during my time of testing.

My dear parents, Albert and Geraldine Smith, who have been my role models. Tough and loving, they spoiled all of us children and gave us the curiosity to go out and conquer the world around us.

I am forever grateful to my whole extended family for their love and support.

Acknowledgments

I want to thank **Lee Porter** for her support and encouragement while I was writing this book. She kept encouraging me to get it done. I thank you, Lee, from the bottom of my heart. This has been a labor of love.

I must acknowledge our dear **Tricia** and her son. They have no idea how God used them in this quest of mine to get the book written. It was their untimely death in December of 2003 that finally set me on this path, and I know they are in Heaven watching me complete it. I simply had to sit down at my computer and begin to write. Never would I have believed the homegoing of two beloved believers would be the catalyst to bring me to this point, but God knows what He is doing.

I must also thank my Pastor, **Carolyn Sissom**. It is not often that one is able to have a pastor who spends time with them on a one-to-one basis, but God has given me such a person in Carolyn. She is an awesome woman of God, always there for me and my family. I have never found anyone like her. She and her family have ministered to me and Craig in such a special and intimate way.

God is so good to have given me such a great pastor, and I pray for her each and every day. I pray that she will be blessed beyond blessed. Together we have had such fun serving the Lord. She has preached, and I have sung on several ministry trips she invited me on. She uses many different psalmists, and I want her to know how grateful I am that she lets me tag along with her. I told her that all I wanted to do is go with her and hold the Bible for her as she preached the Word. No greater honor could be bestowed on me. I am a bondservant to the Lord Jesus Christ, and I count it all joy. I love you, Carolyn, woman of God,

I have two very special friends in my life that I thank God for every day. They are **Karen Bovett** and **Marcia Feldt**. Without their love and support and kindness to me, my life would be not be nearly as full. I am so thankful to God for giving me such wonderful and loving friends.

I have known these two ladies for twenty-three years. God set them in my life when everyone else either turned away or just didn't want to spend time with me while I was going through the fire. I am happy to say that I have won. I passed the test, and now I thank God for giving me this opportunity to keep traveling down this journey of life with two such beautiful women. I love you both.

Contents

Dear Reader 11
Introduction 13

1. Tragedies Come and Tragedies Go 17
2. Houston, Here I Come, Ready or Not 21
3. Life Is a Play, and Life Is My Playground 25
4. Turned Out But Turned On 33
5. Dungeon of Despair 41
6. The Blessings of Having a Child 45
7. Footloose and Fancy Free 49
8. Music Heals Me 53
9. Angel of Light or Angel of Lies? 59
10. Ironing Is a Drag, But Bring on the Heat 63
11. There Is a Price to Pay 67
12. Meeting Ruth Ward Heflin 71
13. Craig Albert Owen 77
14. The School of the Holy Spirit 81
    In Conclusion 83
    Author Contact Page 86

And we know that all things work together for good to them that love God, to them who are the called according to his purpose.
— **ROMANS 8:28**

Dear Reader

Never would I have ever believed I would be writing a book about my life. When the Lord Jesus Christ entered my life, I was a very worldly woman. Now, my goal is to share the Good News with everyone I come in contact with. Life is so short, and we are here for such a short time. Then, we get to meet God and live in His Heaven for eternity. What a day that will be! I look forward to it.

May the Lord richly bless everyone who reads this book of mine. I pray blessings on each of you as you take the time to open it and read what happened to me and what brought me to the saving knowledge of Jesus Christ, the real Jesus, not the counterfeit Jesus that so many cults aspire to follow.

Maybe there is someone out there who needs to read this account of what happened to me.

Having the Time of My Life

Never in my dreams would I have believed Mormonism would bring me to the truth of finding the true Jesus Christ of the Word of God, but that's what happened.

Again, life is short. Make each day count, hold short accounts, and don't hold grudges. We don't walk in anyone else's shoes but our own. I surely do not know all the answers, but I do know who holds all those answers. He is Jesus Christ, my ONE AND ONLY TRUE LOVE.

Introduction

This is my story, how I came to the saving knowledge of Jesus Christ. I put this labor of love off for many years, but finally God spoke to me very clearly: "This is the time," and I got started writing.

Finally sitting down at the computer and putting the words on paper, as it were, was sparked by a horrible tragedy. One of my sisters in Christ, Tricia, along with one of her sons, was killed by an intruder coming into her home after she had come home from an outing with her family. This devastated me. My heart was heavy as I wrote the words that follow, but I knew that out of great tragedy comes victory.

Tricia and her son are now walking on the streets of Glory in the presence of Almighty God, and no matter how they got there, they got there.

Praise be to God in all things. Not necessarily *for* all things, but *IN* ALL THINGS.

I want to thank many people for pushing me to begin this journey. First and foremost, my husband Craig, and my daughter, Kelly Noel Amussen. Then there were the many intercessors who prayed me through every tight spot on this walk.

This journey, by no means, has been a lone walk. Many of us are walking this path today, some in single motherhood, some alone, and others married. My journey took me far from my roots. I was rebellious in my youth, but the Lord got me by the collar and redirected my life for His glory. Maybe you can relate to this story.

I am not unique, but unique to God. He made us all very special and unique in design. Nothing escapes His eyes. Nothing! And no one escapes His presence. God is a good God.

Come now, join me on this journey as I relate my story. I can promise you this: after reading my story, you will come away saying, "She is either crazy or she really did find God." Believe me, I found God, the one true God, the Rose of Sharon, the Great King, the Lord God Almighty,

Introduction

the Prince of Peace, the Everlasting Father. He is all of that and more. May God be praised for His love for me and for all of us living in this time He has ordained for us.

Enjoy reading! I declare to you that the words of this book are a true and accurate account of my life story, giving the Lord Jesus Christ all the glory. None for me, but all for Him. Praise His holy name. Amen!

Helen Smith Owen
San Antonio, Texas

Chapter 1

Tragedies Come and Tragedies Go

The LORD is my shepherd; I shall not want. He maketh me to lie down in green pastures: he leadeth me beside the still waters. He restoreth my soul: he leadeth me in the paths of righteousness for his name's sake. Yea, though I walk through the valley of the shadow of death, I will fear no evil: for thou art with me; thy rod and thy staff they comfort me. Thou preparest a table before me in the presence of mine enemies: thou anointest my head with oil; my cup runneth over. Surely goodness and mercy shall follow me all

Having the Time of My Life

the days of my life: and I will dwell in the house of the LORD for ever.   Psalm 23

TRAGEDIES COME AND TRAGEDIES GO. MY STORY starts when I was a young girl living with a tribe of people known as my family. I am the oldest of six brother and sisters, three girls and three boys. We had fun growing up. The things we did as kids were so innocent. Today things do not seem quite as simple as those lazy days we were growing up in Port Arthur, Texas. We were not touched with crime, not in our neighborhood. Texas, in those days, was carefree and fun.

Mom and Dad took wonderful care of their brood of curious and smart children. We all tried to get their attention. Me … I tried anyway I could.

My brothers always had pets and were always into everything normal boys were into. My little sisters were so precious. They shared a room with each other, so they were very close. I, on the other hand, was the oldest, so that meant I got my own room.

I was the loner, the outcast, and felt set apart from everyone else in a way. Little did I know

Tragedies Come and Tragedies Go

at the time, but this was God training me for something He had chosen me for.

I never excelled in school, except in music. I always made A's in music, C's in math, A's in English, and low C's in Geometry. Any math, forget it. That was not my bag at all. But curiosity was my gift. I loved finding out the truth of things and was always asking questions, always exploring new horizons. That is what led me to Jesus Christ. Was He some fairy tale person, or was He who He claimed to be? That was the sixty-four-thousand-dollar question.

I won some awards in high school, but the outstanding gift I saw in myself was an ability to see people as special. People are special. They have gifts and talents. Many of them don't believe in themselves, but I always cared about making people feel special and loved.

When God came into this equation, He developed this gift much further. It's not that I don't have enemies. Like everyone else, I do. Because I'm so honest and open with my feelings, some people don't like that part of my personality. Maybe it has something to do with the fact that I can read a person quite well. It's a gift.

Having the Time of My Life

I used to think I might be clairvoyant or psychic, but God showed me that this type of activity was not from Him in any way, shape, or form. As I matured and got older, I realized that someone was leading me down a path, and it was not a good path. I didn't understand what this was all about.

All through my college years, Martha (a high school and college classmate) and I would go to a fortuneteller. We really thought this woman could tell us things about ourselves that no one else knew. That was a big mistake. BIG!

I was the wild one in the family, but *rebellious* was a new term to me. I thought I was just being independent and motivated, but that was not the case at all. Something was leading me on a path of destruction, and I didn't understand what that was ... not until 1978.

Chapter 2

Houston, Here I Come, Ready or Not

Turn us again, O God of hosts, and cause thy face to shine; and we shall be saved.
                                    Psalm 80:7

MOVING TO HOUSTON WAS AN EXPERIENCE IN itself. I had just come home from Stockholm, Sweden, after having spent my last year of college studies there. All the fun I had and all the wonderful things I got to do ... I owe it all to my parents for allowing it. Traveling all across Europe for those ten months and studying the Swedish language paid off. Later in life, it would be a blessing knowing how to relate to people of all walks of life. That experience greatly broadened my understand of people, and I always loved being around people.

Houston was such a big city compared to little Port Arthur. I had suddenly come into my own.

As an oil town, Houston was booming in the 1970s and 80s, and because it was big, there were lots of things going on. It wasn't long before I got into the dating scene.

I had run off with a high school sweetheart and married this fellow. As it turned out, I couldn't stand him. His mom was Catholic and very old-fashioned Catholic. I got to where I couldn't stand her, and she couldn't stand me. I had taken her little boy away from her, and I was not Catholic. That was a big deal in those days. I'm so glad I got rid of that man. He was holding me back from my destiny. (More about him in another chapter.)

Here I was, freshly home from Stockholm, Sweden, and I landed a very good teaching job with a wonderful, godly principal. He was a good man, and he taught me many things. He had come from the military, so he ran his school like his own military post. I needed that training and discipline. I called my time there my boot camp.

Houston, Here I Come, Ready or Not

I was with this principal for three years, and then I moved on down the road to another school, one less structured. Always, however, I managed to find people I loved teaching with, kids I adored teaching, and parents who appreciated my hard work.

Traveling to Europe was my outlet. I would save my money and each summer head back to Europe to see my friends in Sweden. I did this four times. My friends over there were so precious to me. All these years I have managed to maintain a relationship with four of them, and I am thankful for their friendship.

During this time, my brothers were doing their own thing. One had gotten married, and they had a baby, and the other two were still in college. My sisters were in college too. My blessed Daddy always had kids in school somewhere across this land. I can't even imagine the cost of sending six kids to college, but by the grace of God, he and Mama did it.

Consequently, we all have college degrees. We earned them, but it was all paid for by our parents' hard work.

Chapter 3

Life is a Play, and Life Is My Playground

Because thou hast made the LORD, which is my refuge, even the most High, thy habitation; there shall no evil befall thee, neither shall any plague come nigh thy dwelling. For he shall give his angels charge over thee, to keep thee in all thy ways. They shall bear thee up in their hands, lest thou dash thy foot against a stone. Thou shalt tread upon the lion and adder: the young lion and the dragon shalt thou trample under feet. Because he hath set his love upon me, therefore will I deliver him: I will set him on high, because he hath known my name. He

*shall call upon me, and I will answer him:
I will be with him in trouble; I will deliver
him, and honour him. With long life will
I satisfy him, and shew him my salvation.*
Psalm 91:9-16

I EXPERIENCED MANY ADVENTURES WHEN I MOVED and settled in Houston, lots of dates, and lots of parties. I was very worldly. I won't give the details here, but suffice it to say that I just did a lot of partying and dating ... until I finally got tired of that life. It eventually became apparent to me that this was a street of no return, or should I say, no heavenly return. There was no eternal value whatsoever in that lifestyle.

I am so glad I was able to escape that life. I literally planned my escape. I was approaching thirty, and I had long wanted to be married and have a baby by that time. Now the clock was ticking, and so was I on the inside. Timing was of the essence. I wanted to settle down and have a family. That was what it came down to. I suddenly thought to myself, "It's time!"

I had met a lovely lady during my teaching days in Pasadena, and she introduced me to a

Life is a Play, and Life Is My Playground

sweet couple. Little did I know that they had a son, Jerry Amussen. Before long, we began dating, and ended up married and me with child.

I gave birth to a beautiful little baby girl, and we named her Kelly Noel. She was not only beautiful; she was such a blessing to my life. I knew she was special from the start. Every day of my pregnancy, I would put my hand over my big belly and thank God for giving me this baby.

Several times I almost lost her. I would start bleeding and have to get to a doctor and have some sort of hormonal shot to stop the bleeding. Kelly is truly a miracle from the Lord.

Here I was, twenty-nine years old and raising a beautiful daughter with a husband whom I adored. What more could I want? But I could not have anticipated what was around the corner. All I wanted was for my daughter and I and my husband to live happily ever after. That's the fairy tale ending, after all, living happily ever after in this play called life.

About six months into the marriage, I noticed that a change was coming over me. I was not happy. I was living with someone who expected me to be very subservient to his every wish. He had an attitude about women that concerned me. What I hadn't known when we married was that he was looking for a Mormon wife, for he had been raised Mormon.

I was not a Mormon, nor did I ever want to be a Mormon. But to make him happy, I now agreed to take lessons in the Mormon Church. I took the lessons, but halfway through them, I met a couple who lived on the next street over. They were Christians, they knew about these "lessons," and they had been praying for me. As it turned out, they had been friends with my husband's first wife.

Very patiently and with much love, this lady would show me in the Bible scriptures that said things like: "no one should add to or take away from the Word of God." She showed me step-by-step and word-by-word, where this was located. Next, she said, "Look at what this says here." I can't remember the exact scripture she was pointing out to me, but it said in essence that it was not from God to have any other books before the one true and living Book, the Holy Bible.

Life is a Play, and Life Is My Playground

At first, I thought it was ludicrous of her to show me all this. I remember asking, "Sandra, do you mean to say you think being a Mormon is of the devil?" She surprised me by agreeing with this statement.

This began my quest to find the truth, to find out if what she was saying was true or was it just her interpretation of the Bible? I had always had a great desire to know the truth about anything and everything. Now I wanted to know where these thoughts were coming from. After all, I had a beautiful little girl to raise. She was the apple of my eye. How could I even entertain the thought of believing the religion of my husband was of the devil?

I had too much to lose by this time. I was married to this man. I had picked him out and made the unconscious decision to have a family with him by the time I was thirty. And now I was in this marriage for the long haul.

I was not about to get another divorce. No way, Jose. That was out of the question for me. But something kept pushing me to find the truth about Mormonism. Was this church good or was it bad? I had to find out.

Having the Time of My Life

As we got closer and closer to the end of the lessons I was taking in the Mormon Church, I noticed something about my husband. He had become very sweet to me again. It was as if he was wanting me to believe his Mormon faith so badly. He was trying so hard to convince me that this was the truth that he had actually changed before my very eyes.

This finally came to a climax one day, and I was desperate to know the truth. I was sick and home alone at the time. I went into the bedroom, and standing right at the door, I looked up toward Heaven and said, "Jesus, I have no idea if this church is of You or not, but will You show me? If it is of You, then I will follow it. I will join the Mormon Church. But if the Mormon Church is NOT of You, please let me know ?"

That was all it took. Immediately I had His answer. I heard the words, "Helen, this is not of Me."

That experience was so real that I will never, ever forget it. Suddenly, things made sense to me. This had to have been the Holy Spirit beginning to work in my life. I knew that I knew

Life is a Play, and Life Is My Playground

that I knew: Mormonism was not of God. That was all I knew, but it was enough.

I didn't know much about the Scriptures, and I could not have explained in detail why I was making this decision. I just knew that the Mormon Church, the Church of the Latter Day Saints, as they call themselves, did not have the answers I was looking for. Now, what was I to do about it? That was the question.

Chapter 4

Turned Out, But Turned On

Create in me a clean heart, O God; and renew a right spirit within me. Psalm 51:10

I USED TO THINK BEING MARRIED TO A MORMON was the worst mistake a woman could ever have made in life, but I have come to regard this season of my life very differently. First, I now had the most beautiful daughter in the world. She was just gorgeous and, in time, she gave her whole heart to the Lord and His will for her life. That alone was worth all the pain, the persecution, and the attacks we both endured during this incredible season of what I refer to as more of my BOOT CAMP EXPERIENCE.

Having the Time of My Life

Boot camp? I don't know much about how the Armed Forces conduct their boot camps, but I do know a little about how the Lord took me on this wild ride, and I had to hang on for dear life.

When you start to get serious about who this Jesus is, get ready for some opposition. If you are truly serious about asking Him who He is, what He does, and what He wants with your life, things will go in a different direction than you planned. Mine did!

When I was a small child, raised in that big tribe of a family, I always wanted to be different. Being the oldest put me in a special position of being the one to go through everything first. Basically, this, to me, was looking for my own identity, and I was willing to do anything to get my parents' attention. God bless their souls, raising this large family had to have been trying and tiring for them both. What a wonderful set of parents I have had all these years! They have stood by each one of us in such a special way.

It is hard now just writing about this. My parents raised very independent-thinking adults. We are all very unique and very special in design. Looking at this now from my perspective, I realize that the

Turned Out, But Turned On

Lord was training me for ministry. Being in this big family was a ministry unto itself. We are all very different and very special individuals. God has gifted each one of us in a special way.

I like to call us a potpourri of God's awesome handiwork. We each possess unique gifts and talents, and growing up, we were always encouraged to find our giftings. But, somehow my giftings and talents of singing were never really encouraged. This was not because my parents were trying to mold me into being an engineering type person, but because they basically didn't understand the music business or anything about ministry, especially a woman being in full time ministry. Horrors! That was not acceptable at all.

Actually, as I was growing up, we never attended church regularly. It was just not something that was on our list of top priorities. But God was not giving up on me. He had a plan all along. And, praise the Lord, I am now walking in that awesome plan He chose for me.

It's amazing to me. We can hinder our walk with the Lord at any age, but the Lord will never stop speaking to us. It doesn't matter how old you are or how handicapped you feel you might be. God still wants to talk to you. He really loves us.

Now, back to that first marriage: when I started my senior year of college, I had already "messed up." I had run off and married an old sweetheart of mine, who turned out to be an abuser. Not understanding the dynamics of adult children of alcoholics and not understanding this insidious disease made me walk into things I wished I never would have walked into.

First of all, alcoholism is a family disease, and it is inherited. If someone you are dating has alcoholism in their family, you'd better watch out. You are in for a life of misery. Misery was that first marriage. Thank the Lord I had the good sense to finally bolt that relationship. It was at least a beginning step to escape this curse.

Now, here I was, twenty-three years old, fresh out of college, and ready for new adventures, and did I find adventures. I had lived in Stockholm, Sweden that full year while attending the Institute for English Speaking Students based out of the University of Stockholm. Oh, what a wonderful year that was! The adventures

Turned Out, But Turned On

and the people I met were, to say the least, awesome.

I not only learned Swedish in two months, but the traveling experience I gained was priceless. You have to remember, this was at the height of the Vietnam War, and Sweden was letting U.S. deserters come into their country for a brief stay. Some ended up staying and marrying Swedish women and becoming Swedish citizens. Some later came back to the States and faced the music. When all was said and done, I was glad I escaped all of that tumult and hid out in Sweden.

Traveling to the European countries was such a treat for me. Learning to snow ski in Badgastein, Austria was the most thrilling of all. My traveling buddy, Karen Johnson, and I would meet up on holidays and travel by rail all over the European countries. We have very fond memories of this time of our lives.

Karen is now working for the Justice Department in Washington, D.C. She has also managed to raise a family of three children. She and her kids have lived all over the world. She is the epitome of what world traveling means.

Having the Time of My Life

What a gutsy woman! She was my traveling buddy for two years in a row.

Looking back on all of this, I would have never realized my dream of travel had it not been for my dad and mom allowing me to do it. I will forever be grateful to them for letting me experience all of this.

My dad received an awesome promotion with Gulf Oil and was transferred to Venezuela. While they were in their first year down there, I was in Sweden, my brothers were studying at Texas A&M, my middle sister was here in the States attending high school, and my baby sister and brother were snuggled closely in Venezuela attending the camp school there. So, we were all scattered, experiencing things we would all have to write about some day. What a blessing this all turned out to be for each of us!

But more was to come. I was getting restless. Now, here I was, twenty-three, coming home from the most exciting year of my young life, and feeling empty to the max. What was wrong with me? I could not put a finger on what was bothering me. I had it all: youth, a good teaching job at the time, lots of traveling experience,

Turned Out, But Turned On

and more planned, a great family, and still I was lost—totally lost and getting more lost as the days went by.

I had to explore this more thoroughly. How was I to go about finding what was missing in my life? Oh, God thank You for protecting me from the evil one. And thank You for watching out for this little waif of a girl.

God had plans for me, big plans. If only I would have listened more closely. But, no, I just kept on the same fast track of living in the world, and it made me feel empty! Empty! Empty!

Chapter 5

Dungeon of Despair

But be not thou far from me, O LORD: O my strength, haste thee to help me. Deliver my soul from the sword; my darling from the power of the dog. Psalm 22:19-20

When I finally got saved and filled with the Holy Spirit, my whole existence changed. It really did. In one instant, I was walking from the kingdom of darkness into the Kingdom of Light, and it was glorious. At first, I could not believe how much God loved me just for me. I didn't have to prove anything to Him. He already knew me, and He accepted me just the way I was. This was so hard for me to understand.

Having the Time of My Life

As I was growing up, I felt like I had to perform in order to get everyone's attention. When this awesome experience happened to me, the first thing I did was get on my knees in my living room and say aloud, "Lord, You really do exist. Forgive me for being a sinner."

No one had led me through the Lord's Prayer, no one, except the Holy Spirit. Now, I looked outside my den window and saw the most beautiful sunshine and saw my little airplane plant hanging in my den. My first thought was, "Lord, You make life so beautiful. You really do."

I thought that was the most beautiful sunshine and the most beautiful little airplane plant I had ever seen. Even the way I looked at nature now was astounding to me. This was my first look at life from the Kingdom of Light, and there was such color in God's majesty.

I am still in awe of how I came to the Lord. It still gives me goose bumps when I think of how He humbled Himself to meet me where I was. What an awesome God!

Everything was now wonderful ... except my marriage. When my husband came home

Dungeon of Despair

from work, all I could talk about was Jesus. He thought I had lost my mind. From then on, for five long years, he and I grew further and further apart, and I grew more in love with the Lord. What a boot camp experience! I am just glad to say that I lived through it.

My dungeon of despair eventually turned into a symphony of praise for the Lord God Almighty. I would eventually start a ministry of singing, and it has been a journey of love through the pain and tragedy of the divorce that would inevitably come.

Another divorce was the last thing I ever wanted, but when the Lord lets you know, "This is the time to go ahead and leave the marriage," then it's time. Listen to the Lord very carefully, loved ones.

It was a labor of love to let that marriage go. I loved my husband very much, but I could not stand the pain of rejection from him because of my stand for Jesus Christ and had to leave. I had to go. In one sense of the word, it seemed like the end of the world, but in reality, it was the beginning of doors opening and adventures waiting to come.

Having the Time of My Life

What a glorious God we serve! He knows what is around every corner of our lives. He came to give us life and life more abundantly. He really loves us and has proven His undying love to me over and over again.

Chapter 6

The Blessings of a Child

Lo, children are an heritage of the Lord: and the fruit of the womb is his reward. As arrows are in the hand of a mighty man; so are children of the youth. Happy is the man that hath his quiver full of them: they shall not be ashamed, but they shall speak with the enemies in the gate. Psalm 127:3-5

GOD WAS SO GRACIOUS TO GIVE ME MY DAUGHTER to raise. She is now in her forties, is serving the Lord, and is on fire for Him. She is just an awesome child of God.

There was a time when things were very unsettled with her, and she seemed to be slipping away to the world. Had it not been for prayer and for my prayer partners in Mary Willis' Bible study, things might have turned out differently. Ladies, if you are in Mary's Bible study, stay there. Do not retreat. Share you prayer needs and trust God.

In the early days of Mary's studies, she would have a huge board for all of us to write our prayer requests on. I was always writing something up there. I wasn't too proud to express my needs. God had humbled me through many experiences.

Looking back, Kelly's name was up there on that board many times, as many other names were, and by the grace of the Lord, through our never-ending quest to hear from the Lord and to expect answers from His throne of grace, His will was done. My daughter not only got saved and Spirit-filled, but she has dedicated her life to serving our King of Kings. It was all a result of putting her name on that prayer board.

I encourage you today, whoever you are, to share your prayer needs with a friend or a Bible study leader and believe God together for the impossible. No one is ever too far away

The Blessings of a Child

from God's grace and mercy. I am living proof of that.

God loves our children, but I am also not so naive as to not know that Satan makes a bid for their souls too. You have to cover yourself with the Word of God to stand and fight this battle. God does the battling for us, if we will just believe His Word and believe Him to accomplish what He has set out to do. And that is to save our kids and to use them for His glory.

God has a destiny for each one of our children. I want His destiny for my life and the life of my family members, and I will fight in prayer and stand and do more praying for each of my family members and loved ones. Life is too short, and prayer is only a breath away.

Prayer changes things. Prayer changes me. Prayer changes world situations. Prayer does the work. And the work is the Lord's. It is His Word and His work. We are just asked to follow His direction and His plans. That is sometimes hard to do, and it takes practice.

Get on your knees or on your face before Him, and cry out to Him for your needs. He will answer. He always does. He might not answer the way we want, but He is always bending down with a listening ear to hear what His kids need.

One year, Lee Porter said to me, in a conversation we were having before Bible study with Mary, that she thought I was an intercessor. I had never heard that term *intercessor* before, but as the years have gone by in my Christian walk, I have come to the conclusion that she was right. That is exactly what I am, an intercessor, one who stands in the gap for others and believes for them in their time of need.

By God's grace, someone stood in the gap for me, and now the gift is the giver. I am standing in the gap for others the Lord tells me to pray for at any given moment, and I do not easily give up. I persevere in prayer until the answer comes.

Chapter 7

Footloose and Fancy Free

Stand fast therefore in the liberty wherewith Christ hath made us free, and be not entangled again with the yoke of bondage.
Galatians 5:1

THIS TITLE EXPLAINS MY JOURNEY ON DOWN THE road as a single Mom. I capitalized the word *Mom* to show the importance of that term.

Mom ... what does that make you think of? It makes me think of the times I was both dad and mom, counselor, car mechanic, chief cook and bottle washer, social director, and program chairman. And, at the same time, I was working full-time as a teacher. Those who have walked in these same steps are to be commended for just even showing up each day for the journey.

There were many days when I wanted to just sit down and cry. It was overwhelming to me to have all this responsibility and be without the kind of money and help I had been used to having. At times, it was really a struggle. As I look back, however, I realize that Kelly and I never hurt for anything. God provided so wonderfully for us during this time in our lives. If we were in need, we didn't know it. We truly had everything provided for us.

I didn't date. That was the key to this period for me. I didn't bring another man into my relationship with Kelly, except for one time, and I was sorry for that one time. But we went on down the road, and I continued in the path God had chosen for me here.

I have great respect for single parents—male or female. I have such a burden for this special role today. It is not an easy job to play both mom and dad to your kids, but we got through it.

I was single almost eight years, and then I met my husband Craig, who was such a sweetheart to us both. He truly became a father to Kelly

Footloose and Fancy Free

and a good husband to me. I cannot say it was all easy, but we maintained our relationship through the good and the bad, Jesus being our glue.

There were days when I thought maybe I had heard wrong about being remarried, but God knows what is around your corner, and He knew what was around mine. The only advice I would like to share is this: Please invite your single friends over for a nice meal. Take them on a vacation with you and your family. Share your life with them. This is so important. God will reward you for this.

We had a family in Orlando, Florida, that did that for us. We would always go to Destin each summer that I was a single parent, and it meant so much to me and Kelly how this family would share their life and vacations with us. I will be forever grateful to them for all their love and support during this time in my life. Their names are Diane and John Lovitz, and they, too had a daughter—Kerry. Our daughters enjoyed each other's company.

Chapter 8

Music Heals Me

Deliver me from bloodguiltiness, O God, thou God of my salvation: and my tongue shall sing aloud of thy righteousness.
                            Psalm 51:14

I HAVE ALWAYS LOVED SINGING. AT MY CHILDHOOD home in Port Arthur, during times when no one else was around, I would start singing around the house. I stayed home and just sang my heart out. I loved it. Music brought something to my soul, a peace and tranquility I can't even describe. Later on in life, God used music to bring about a major transformation in me.

In high school, I had always been in some of the musicals, but as a dancer, never as a lead singer. I was always just in the background, as one of the chorus dancers. Then, of course, all of the dancers and the actors sang together.

It was not until 1979 that I got a chance to sing for my very first Bible study held in Houston. What an honor to do this for the Lord! I had always loved singing, but after I got saved, I really loved doing it.

I began to sing for the Lord and to the Lord. I made up songs to sing to Him and give Him the glory that only He deserves. Praise His holy name.

About 1986, I joined the Exchange Club of Memorial-Houston, and they began to use my voice for their district conventions and then for some of their national conventions. In essence, God was letting me have fun. I flew all over the country singing for those wonderful conventions.

I loved getting my music together, I loved practicing it, and then I had so much fun performing it, and it was all paid for. God provided everything for this. What a blessing it was!

Not only did I get to sing for the Exchange Club, but later on, the Lord let me go to California

Music Heals Me

and sing for another service organization. That truly blessed me too. I still sing for weddings, Bible studies, and conventions ... anywhere the Lord leads. This is what I enjoy doing the most.

Through all the persecutions, the heartaches, and the tribulations, He has restored my soul, and He does it continually through my singing.

I want my message to come through loud and clear. I belong to Jesus Christ and no one else. Nothing can take me away from His love.

I remember one time especially that He provided supernaturally like never before. I had received an invitation to sing for one of the district Gulf Coast conventions to be held in San Antonio. At the time, money was tight, so I was praying and asking the Lord to help me in this area. I was wondering how in the world I was going to have enough money to go.

Usually, these organizations take care of your room and board and your flight, but I was driving to San Antonio this time, so I would need about $200 for my incidental expenses.

I was sitting in my home one day, and a knock came at the door. A very nice looking man walked up and asked me the strangest question.

He asked if I would mind keeping his golf cart at my home. At the time, I lived in Quail Valley in their cottages section. The cottages had a little golf cart garage with an electrical outlet to recharge the batteries. I was surprised by his request, but I told him, "Of course," he could keep it at my place. He asked if, in exchange for this, I would accept $200 for my trouble. I told him, "That would not be a problem." He handed me the money. Then, he disappeared, and I never saw him again. He did leave me his card.

I went on to San Antonio and sang, and it was a wonderful experience. I needed exactly the amount this man had given me for the trip. The amazing thing was that when I got back home, I wanted to call him and ask why he hadn't brought his golf cart to my home to keep it there. When I called the number on the card he left with me, I was told that no one by that name was at that company. And, they said, no one by that name had ever worked for their company. I kept explaining that I had just met the man, and he gave me his card. I felt so foolish.

After I got to thinking about the whole thing, the Lord put it on my heart that He had sent an angel to help me out financially. I just know it was an angel. Praise the Lord!

There are many more stories about angels that I could tell, but that one is the most awesome, I do believe. God uses angels to meet His kids and their needs. He will send angels to take charge over you. Trust me on this.

Chapter 9

Angel of Light, Angel of Lies?

As for me, I will call upon God; and the Lord shall save me. Evening, and morning, and at noon, will I pray, and cry aloud: and he shall hear my voice. He hath delivered my soul in peace from the battle that was against me: for there were many with me. God shall hear, and afflict them, even he that abideth of old. Selah. Because they have no changes, therefore they fear not God. He hath put forth his hands against such as be at peace with him: he hath broken his covenant. The words of his mouth were smoother than butter, but war was in his heart: his words were softer than oil, yet were they drawn swords. Cast thy burden upon the Lord, and he

Having the Time of My Life

shall sustain thee: he shall never suffer the righteous to be moved. Psalm 55:16-22

BACK WHEN I WAS TAKING THE LESSONS IN THE Mormon Church to appease my then husband, I sensed that something different was about to take place in my life and change my whole perspective. Little did I know that the Lord was preparing me for such an amazing journey.

At first, I had been very excited to be learning something new. I had always loved learning new things, always had a curiosity about life that was sometimes unquenchable. I had always wanted to push the envelope. God took me through this experience, allowing it, that down the road He night get glory from it. If you are stuck in a place, a desert, the backside of the desert, then God is preparing to use you for His Kingdom glory. Trust me on this. It is no accident or mistake that you are in this stuck situation. Look for what God has for you.

When I began reading the Book of Mormon, confused thoughts began to surface. I listened

Angel of Light, Angel of Lies?

intently to the missionaries who would come and present their "gospel" about Joseph Smith and how an angel of light had come to him, showed him some golden plates, and told him that all the other churches were wrong. The angel said he had come to set Joseph Smith free to start a whole new church system.

In my opinion, this was a demonic revelation, and Satan used an angel of light, his angel of light, to trick Joseph Smith. Instead of an angel of light, I call him the angel of lies.

Deceit is a tricky word. When you are deceived, you usually never know you're being deceived until after the fact. What helped me through this was that I had the curiosity to search for the truth about a situation or a person. That person was Joseph Smith.

I concluded, on my own, without any legal scholars to present their case to me, that Joseph Smith had been a liar and a cheat. God was beginning to work in my life at this point. Someone was praying for me to find the truth about Mormonism and Joseph Smith, and I was beginning to listen to God.

This strong opinion about Mormonism and its leaders did not serve me well at home. My husband eventually left me and our daughter for bigger and better pastures, but this was the turning point of our marriage. God used this foundation to further my walk with Him in later years.

I stand by my declaration here: Joseph Smith and his minions have done more harm to innocent people searching for God than any other cult in existence today.

God does have a plan. Never ever forget this one fact: He really does love His kids. Just give Him a chance in your life. Call out to Him. Get on your face before Him and ask Him for help. He will always show up in your life if you let Him. That's what He did for me.

I cried out for God to take me out of the mess I had walked into, and He did it. Praise His holy name forever and ever.

Chapter 10

Ironing Is a Drag, but Bring on the Heat

God standeth in the congregation of the mighty; he judgeth among the gods. How long will ye judge unjustly, and accept the persons of the wicked? Selah. Defend the poor and fatherless: do justice to the afflicted and needy. Deliver the poor and needy: rid them out of the hand of the wicked. They know not, neither will they understand; they walk on in darkness: all the foundations of the earth are out of course. I have said, Ye are gods; and all of you are children of the most High. But ye shall die like men, and fall like one of the princes. Arise, O God, judge the earth: for thou shalt inherit all nations.

Psalm 82:1-8

THE FIRST THING I MUST ADMIT TO YOU HERE IS THAT I don't like being put in the fiery furnace of affliction. It's no fun. Nor do I recommend it. But God chose to take me this way, and I went at His call. So I'm here to declare that He knows what He's doing. If you are going through a hard time in your life, count it all joy. God has a reason for allowing it.

The years I was locked away with the Lord were the years He spoke to me very clearly. I got to know Him very intimately. By studying His Word, by hanging onto every little sermon I heard during the eight-year trial period, I learned not only how to hear from God; I also learned how to pray for other people and for their needs.

Teaching school during this time was difficult, but somehow, by God's grace, I got through it, and so did my daughter. I'm sure one of these days she will write her own documentary of what it was like for her going through this.

Ironing Is a Drag, but Bring on the Heat

I used to feel very guilty having her go through this with me, but what else could I do? I released all the guilt and anxiety I felt about this and gave it to the Lord, for Him to use however He pleases.

When heat is applied to metal, it bends, and I started bending. Iron sharpens iron, and it did this for me. I learned about myself early on. I saw some ugly and unsightly things in myself that I did not like. I saw how I had misjudged people and how I had hurt them.

The turning point finally came when I realized I had no control over anything. Nothing! God had control over me and my future. He was in the driver's seat of my life.

During this time, I lost a lot of so-called friends, friends who had started out with me, but when the heat was turned up in my life, they started running the other way. All except one person—Karen Bovett. Karen stood by me through this ordeal as a good soldier, an awesome prayer partner, and a devoted friend. We shall forever remain connected through this.

The good Lord loves you like no one else can. He will change your life very quickly ... if and when He sees that you want Him badly enough. You might have to walk through some fire, but He will bring you out on the other side without even a hair on your head being singed.

Looking back, I would not trade this training camp for anything. I am still in training, as we all are. No one has arrived, and if they tell you they have, be careful. Only the Lord can bring you through the furnace of your own afflictions, and you must trust Him to do it His way.

Chapter 11

There Is a Price to Pay

And when Jesus was entered into Capernaum, there came unto him a centurion, beseeching him, and saying, Lord, my servant lieth at home sick of the palsy, grievously tormented.

And Jesus saith unto him, I will come and heal him.

The centurion answered and said, Lord, I am not worthy that thou shouldest come under my roof: but speak the word only, and my servant shall be healed. For I am a man under authority, having soldiers under me: and I say to this man, Go, and he goeth; and to another, Come, and he cometh; and to my servant, Do this, and he doeth it.

Having the Time of My Life

When Jesus heard it, he marvelled, and said to them that followed, Verily I say unto you, I have not found so great faith, no, not in Israel. And I say unto you, That many shall come from the east and west, and shall sit down with Abraham, and Isaac, and Jacob, in the kingdom of heaven. But the children of the kingdom shall be cast out into outer darkness: there shall be weeping and gnashing of teeth.

And Jesus said unto the centurion, Go thy way; and as thou hast believed, so be it done unto thee. And his servant was healed in the selfsame hour. Matthew 8:5-13

WHEN I FINALLY DECIDED TO GO AHEAD AND divorce Jerry, it was with much trepidation. First of all, it says in the Word of God that the sins of the father will be passed on to the third and fourth generation. That is very true, and I took that scripture very seriously. But I had no choice. This man was not in love with me, nor did he even like me as a person. Period!

It was so sad, but I really believe his heart was hardened as Pharaoh's heart was hardened

There Is a Price to Pay

toward the Israelites in Egypt during the time of the great Exodus. No amount of my talking him out of this divorce went anywhere. He was determined to see things his way, and that was to leave our union. For whatever reason, God used this to help me get to where He wanted me to go. He wanted me serving Him, and one cannot serve two masters at the same time. It was either God or mammon, and I chose God.

The amount of tears shed during this time was tremendous. I wept and kept pouring this out to God each day. How could He use me if I was divorced? Well, beloved He uses whom He chooses, and that fear was something I had to finally be released from.

This mindset that God could not bless a person like me because I was divorced is what religious people put in front of me. They kept reminding me: "How can God use you if you've been divorced? You cannot be used to sing either." That is what I heard again and again. Well, I am here to tell you that those people are in bondage to religion. God does use willing vessels, no matter how they have "messed up" in the past. Trust me, if someone is telling you something like this, go the other way. Forgive them for their stupidity and just go on down the road. You might have to go it alone, but just keep your eyes on Jesus, and He will direct your path.

For those who are reading this, God is no respecter of persons. He uses whom He chooses to use. Period! Just have a willing heart for Him. And just keep keeping on in your walk with Him. It might get pretty muddy along the way, but just keep moving forward. You might have to change churches, you might have to change friends, and you might have to change cities or jobs, but just keep keeping on. Do not look to the left nor to the right. Just keep your eyes on Jesus Christ.

I think the most wonderful thing is taking place in my heart as I document this whole story. I am being delivered of unforgiveness for people who tried to stop my ministry. I am truly moving now in the giftings God has placed in me, and He can do this for you, too. It might take years for you to come out and see the fruits of your prayers for your life and for the lives of others, but your giftings will be used by God. That is what He does because He loves His kids.

Chapter 12

Sister Ruth Ward Heflin

My soul shall be satisfied as with marrow and fatness; and my mouth shall praise thee with joyful lips.   Psalm 63:5

OVER THE YEARS, I HAVE ALWAYS MANAGED TO FIND the time and the money to travel. In my last ten years of ministry, God has opened some pretty awesome doors to me to walk through, all having to do with Him. After being in the Exchange Club and singing for their national conventions and district conventions, it was time to move on down the road. I loved being with all my fellow Exchangites, but I knew when it was time to close that door and go on to other things. This happened in 1999.

Having the Time of My Life

At the beginning of that year, I felt a call of a different sort on life. God was calling me to pray and fast for our country and its leaders. An old friend of mine from Women's Aglow called me and asked me to speak at one of their meetings about prayer. I did, and it was glorious. I had just returned from a trip to Washington, D.C. and had been invited to join a group of people heavy into Campus Crusades for Christ. It was the first prayer and fasting conference sponsored by this great organization. I immediately knew this was God.

We had just sold our big half-million dollar home in Bellaire, and it felt pretty easy to let it go. I had other things on my mind. I wanted to go to D.C. and pray and fast for our country. God will use you ... if you will submit to Him totally, and that's what I did. I gave Him my time, I gave Him my talents, and I asked Him to use me as He saw fit. Get ready, for when you do this, He will take you up on your offer.

He also let me go to some pretty awesome seminars during this time all over the country about intercessory prayer. I met many wonderful, strong intercessors all over this country, and

Sister Ruth Ward Heflin

they introduced me to a deeper walk with the Lord. From California to Florida, I met some of the most awesome intercessors ever, and they truly taught me what it means to stand in the gap for our country as a whole.

I also met Sister Ruth Heflin at her campground in Ashland, Virginia in 1999 for the very first time. What an awesome prayer warrior and woman of God! I had never met anyone quite like her. She ran the campground which was begun by her parents in the early 1950s. It is called Calvary Pentecostal Campground. Ministers from all denominations come to this place to worship, to get refreshed, and to just be there for others. I have never been to such an anointed place.

Ruth's parents were early Pentecostal pioneers. One of the leaders of the National Day of Prayer in Houston introduced me to her. I had never met such a woman. Marietta Maxfield told me all about how she received what she called "gold dust" all over her as she preached up in Virginia that summer. I had never heard of such a strange thing in my life.

At first, I thought the gold dust might be fake, but who would do such a trick? So, being the curious sort of person I am, I decided to go see for myself what this was all about. That is what brought me to the camp that year, to find more of the Lord, and to see and hear about this "gold dust."

Well, I found, not only more of the Lord on this campground, but I felt such a deep presence of the Lord there. The meetings were held twice daily, and I went to every meeting I could. Sister Heflin was at these meetings, but she was very ill at the time. So, another sister in the Lord preached the messages. I was so taken with the place. I felt such a deep presence of the Lord in the meetings that I did not want to leave the place.

As I was sitting in the first meeting after arriving, gold dust started appearing on my hands and all over my face. I shouted for joy. It just happened, and it continued to do so the whole time I was in those meetings. That's how I found out about the "gold dust." It was a manifestation of God's presence.

After I came back home, it kept happening. I would be sitting in church in the back and praying, and it would appear all over my hands. I

Sister Ruth Ward Heflin

kept showing it to my husband, Craig, and he was amazed too. How could I tell my church what was happening to me? I decided not to say a word.

I was so hungry for more of the presence of God that I returned to camp three more times during the early 1990s. Then Sister Heflin went to be with the Lord in 2000. I had the privilege of meeting her nine months before she left this earth. What a woman!

I did not understand it all, but God is showing Himself all over this world in signs and wonders. It took a while for this to absorb into my spirit. I had been such a skeptic, but now I know it's real. I don't seek the gift but the Giver. The Giver of all good gifts is Jesus Christ, the real Jesus Christ.

Chapter 13

Craig Albert Owen

For the husband is the head of the wife, even as Christ is the head of the church: and he is the saviour of the body. Ephesians 5:23

I MET CRAIG IN 1990 WHEN I WAS IN THE DEPTHS OF despair. I had just decided to sell my cottage in Quail Valley and move up to Magnolia and teach school. My ex-husband had just remarried, so I was ready to make some drastic changes in my living arrangements and that of my daughter, Kelly. I kept thinking that God would put me and Jerry back together, but it was not to be.

I had waited on him, thinking he would come back to us and realize the horrible mistake he had made by divorcing me. But God had a different plan than I knew about. Looking back, I am so thankful that my life took the pleasant turn it took in meeting my cutie pie husband, Craig Albert Owen.

Craig was a man of many talents, and golf was one of those talents. We had more fun traveling around this country and just being together. He made me laugh, and God knew I needed to laugh and love again. When you have been living in a cave with a cult, life does not seem so happy. But after I walked on down the road, trusting the God of the Bible for my future, life began to look beautiful again. And it still does.

Craig was a survivor. We survived financial ruin, we survived family crises, we survived raising teenage daughters, and we survived each other. God knows what He's doing when you turn your life and marriage over to Him.

Of course, I can't say that life became a bed of roses, but even through the thorns, God was kind to both of us.

I loved my husband more than he knew. I am a big baby half the time, I want my way, and I make noise about it. But, more than anything, Craig was my partner. We learned to live one day at a time, and we learned that every day with each other was a gift.

I also learned to accept Craig for who he was. If he wanted to go play a round of golf, I let him go. He let me go all over the States to prayer conferences and other meetings, for singing or whatever I loved doing. He let me go because he understood that this was part of my personality.

I am forever grateful that he came into my life at just the right time. May we all be so ready to face the future with a good partner. May the good Lord continue to bless us and let us enjoy this incredible ride He has planned for our marriages.

During our twenty-eight years of marriage, I woke up each day excited and smelled the roses in our life. Then, in September of 2017, Craig Albert Owen passed from this life. We miss him.

Chapter 14

The School of the Holy Spirit

God is gone up with a shout, the LORD with the sound of a trumpet. Psalm 47:5

WHEN I BEGAN THIS WALK OF MINE WITH THE Lord, I learned one thing that I shall never, ever forget. I learned that no matter how old one is in the Lord, we are all still learning. We are still in school, so to speak. I call it THE SCHOOL OF THE HOLY SPIRIT because only God's Holy Spirit can direct our path toward Jesus Christ and His righteousness.

I want to live a good life, a life filled with fun and adventure, with Him being my Pilot. Not my will, but His be done in my life from now on.

Having the Time of My Life

Beloved, if you are reading this today, don't hesitate to stop and give your life to God. Ask Him to come in and take control of your life, your family, your job, your work, your play. This will be the best decision you have ever made. Relationships will begin to change for you. You will be set free from the past and from hurts you may have been carrying for decades. Life is to be enjoyed, not to be a binding.

I lived with a lot of fear before asking the Lord into my life. Now, I know beyond a shadow of a doubt, that my life is better than it has ever been. Challenges have come, but God says that He will deliver us out of them ALL.

We might have to go through some pretty hairy things while down here on planet Earth, but beloved, don't give up on Jesus Christ. May the Lord honor and bless your going in and coming out. May He be the shining Light in your life and the life of your family. We can't lose with Jesus being on our side. Praise His name forever and ever.

In Conclusion

In conclusion, I want to write this to all of my loved ones, family, friends, enemies, and acquaintances: Life is so short. If the Lord decides to call me home soon, I will gladly lay down my life for Him in a New York second. But I wanted to leave a written word behind, just in case this becomes the rule. My whole life, up until about 1989, was spent trying to keep up with the Joneses.

I spent a good part of my life as a single mom. That, I would not change for anything. I learned in those days how to lean on the Lord for all my needs and for the needs of my daughter. God provided so beautifully for us during those days. This was the time I learned to pray, and I mean pray.

Never had I needed a thing in my life up until this time. Things were so easily given to me. Life was one big party. But, only in the perspective of a world view, devoid of God and His Word. I thought I knew the Lord. I really thought this. But what He brought me through, oh beloved, now I know Him better, very intimately. He speaks to me, and I sure do listen to Him now.

Make no mistake, one of these days your faith may be tested and tried in the fires of affliction like mine. It happens to us all. We are never beyond His reach. He loves us and wants a relationship with each of His kids. And that includes you and me, beloved. Trust Him no matter what happens in your life. Turn to Him and His Word. Find other believers who will lift you up and support you. Get involved in a Bible study and stay connected with God's people.

I am not speaking about religious people. I'm talking about true believers who have been tested and tried in the fires of affliction. God is able to deliver you out of them all. He has shown me His great love for me and my loved ones. I wonder where I would be had I not turned to the King of Kings. Probably dead and in Hell.

In Conclusion

I loved Pastor E.V. Hill.[1] He told it like it was. He once said that he wanted to go to Heaven because he did not want to go to Hell. And you know why? He said it was because there were no exits in Hell. You could not go and spend a weekend in Hell and then decide you wanted to leave that horrible place. Once in Hell, you will always be in Hell for ETERNITY. That doesn't sound like a good deal to me, and it didn't to him either.

How about you? Are you ready to take some drastic steps and turn to the ONE AND ONLY, JESUS CHRIST. May I be the one to lead you to Him? Cry out to Him. It's so easy to do. Just humble yourself and ask Him to come into your life and take control over all of it. Beloved, this is the best decision you will ever, ever, ever make in your life.

I love you,
Helen Smith Owen

---

[1]. Senior Pastor of Mount Zion Missionary Baptist Church in Los Angeles, California from 1961 until his death, under his leadership it became one of the largest African-American congregations in the U.S. (Wikipedia)

Author Contact

You may correspond directly with the author, Helen Smith Owen, at:

warriorwomen77@gmail,com

And we know that all things work together for good to them that love God, to them who are the called according to his purpose.

– ROMANS 8:28

www.ingramcontent.com/pod-product-compliance
Lightning Source LLC
Chambersburg PA
CBHW031655040426
42453CB00006B/312